How to Host a Party

for 125,000 of Your Closest Friends!

**Turning People into Friends
and Friends into Customers**

**Brad C. Engel
Neil F. Anderson**

How to Host a Party

for 125,000 of Your Closest Friends!

For information about this title or to order other books
and/or electronic media, contact the publisher:

Bethel1808
Lewisville, TX 75057
Bethel1808.com
ISBNs for How to Host a Party
Softcover: 978-1-947201-12-5
eBook: 978-1-947201-13-2
Printed in the United States of America

~ II ~

Dedicated to

*My wonderful wife, Dorothy;
and our great children:
Mark, Nicholas, Trent and
Melissa;
Without their love, support, prayers and originality, this
book would have never happened.*

Neil

*Lauren, my favorite daughter,
who makes friends with everybody, everywhere.
I have always loved being your friend.*

Brad

Acknowledgements

We would like to extend a huge Thank You to our friend and editor, LuAnne Golden. You do such an incredible job and keep us looking so good. Thank you for all your help on this project. You are such a blessing to us.

Contents

~ VIII ~

Foreword

I met Brad Engel and Neil Anderson when I was the guest speaker at an event in 2017. It was a short connection that I probably wouldn't have remembered if it hadn't been for their book, <u>Limitless Connections</u>. This book is filled with incredible ways to network, many of which I implement in my own life and business. Shortly after that event, Brad and Neil reached out to set up a meeting, or what they might call "a party" for us at my office. It was a busy day, but I wanted to give them a couple of minutes of my time. Twenty minutes later, we were having so much fun that I called a couple of other people from the office in to meet with us and we all agreed that we wanted Brad and Neil to speak at our 2018 FASTSIGNS Outside Sales Summit.

When I started in my career, I realized very quickly that everything rises and falls on relationships, so I have spent years developing a mentoring style of leadership. I like to have meetings one-on-one and truly connect with people. This is what Brad and Neil call "having a party"...and they are right. If we make the time that we spend with people enjoyable, then they will want to spend more time with us and eventually become our friends. I love the idea of our customers being treated as friends. Brad and Neil have written another great book: How to Host a Party for 125,000 of Your Closest Friends. This wonderful book is all about how to turn people into friends, and friends into customers.

There are all kinds of sales training and techniques available that work incredibly well and can make us successful, but if we want to be significant in the future, we have to build relationships. That is why I love franchising. I get to build relationships with people and help them achieve the American dream, owning their own business, and being in business for themselves, but not by themselves. They then have the opportunity to build wealth for their families, create economic output and develop their employees. I get to be personally involved in their life and even more importantly, they want me there. I want everybody around me to enjoy the time they spend with me, almost as if they have been to "the party" and this book will teach you how to host a party for each and every person you meet.

I hope to be remembered by all the people I've come in contact with as being someone who made a difference in their lives because I did something caring and loving. I want to meet more people. I want to make more friends and I want to host more parties.

Catherine Monson
President and CEO
FASTSIGNS International, Inc

~ X ~

Introduction

What do you think of when you hear the word "networking?" Maybe you see yourself in the midst of a group of people all exchanging business cards. Maybe you think of all the people who you can try to reach through great communication skills. I used to always exhale a breath of resistance. I knew that I was going to have to find people to meet, smile, introduce myself, smile, be interested, exchange business cards, smile, email, call, smile, write, invite, thank, be courteous, meet again, smile and eventually try to close the deal, knowing full well that they already knew what I did and were not interested. After all my intense work was complete, I had to deal with all the people who got my business card and were trying to network me.

Like most people, I developed a powerful sales resistance. I was in sales, but I hated it when somebody tried to sell to me. So much of this was due to my own corrupt view of sales, business and most importantly...networking.

I was "Doing It Wrong!"

I may technically have been networking, but I was doing it improperly. I was meeting lots and lots of people, but they were just that...initial meetings. Networking was part of my job, but in all honesty, it produced very little return. Of course, I resisted this belief and just went on thinking that I was fantastic at networking. The problem was that I had never really been taught how to actually network.

In the following pages, you will find a different way of networking. A way of networking that will no longer be a chore; a way of networking that will excite and encourage you to want to keep doing it and do it so much better; a way of networking that will feel more like a party, not just for you, but also for your customers, clients and friends.

I first learned what I thought was networking when I was in the insurance business. Nobody taught me how to network. I just went to networking events and simply followed what others did or even just tried to do what came naturally. I assumed that networking should look natural, feel natural, and be natural...but in all honesty, I didn't want to be there. I didn't want to meet new people, and I didn't want to hear the word "No" any more. There was nothing natural about what I was doing. But, I kept trying and eventually became good at my version of networking.

This book is a story about how I came to the realization of what networking truly is and the fact that I had no clue as to what I was doing. When I learned the true art of networking, it changed my life both professionally, and personally. My business friendships became much better; my friendships with neighbors became richer; and people began enjoying being around me. I actually had people calling to ask me to go to lunch. And of course, my sales began to climb and climb.

But this book isn't just about sales. It isn't just about connections. And it isn't just about having meetings. It's about networking as a lifestyle. It's about living a life that other people want to be a part of...a party.

You are about to experience a new kind of party. One in which people will want to come to; one in which people will call you and ask you for; one in which you are the fantastic host to 125,000 of your closest friends. Now...

R.S.V.P

Répondez s'il vous plaît.

At the end of each chapter, you will have an opportunity to R.S.V.P. or respond...not to the authors of this book, but to yourself and to the information you are receiving.

Take these action steps and watch the transformation that happens in your business, your relationships and perhaps most importantly, in you.

Now...

The Party Pooper

Years ago I attended a networking event that, for me, was different. There was actually nothing spectacular about this event compared to any other. I used to joke with myself about how each event I went to was "another event that I wouldn't remember." This one started out the same but became a networking event that I would actually never forget. We were gathered at a museum and supposed to enjoy browsing as we met other people who also were supposed to meet us. I had just finished a long day and was really not in the mood to smile any more that day. I just needed to be done and start again the next day. But, as I was driving home from work, I decided at the last minute to go ahead and make an appearance. Then, I could tell my boss that I attended, in the event that he asked.

I slowly dragged myself from the parking lot to the sidewalk. I remember wondering if networking was really part of my job or if it was considered "over and above." I didn't get paid extra for it, but it was still expected. I would often fluctuate from my "take no prisoners" salesman-mindset to my "I'm feeling underpaid" hourly-mindset. This was one of those fluctuations. I eventually pulled myself together, straightened my shirt, and about fifty feet from the door, I instantly transformed into my alter ego--Networking Man. I didn't have a cape, spandex or even a mask, but my superpower was in full working order. I could network with the best of them. I knew all the catch-phrases and questions to ask that would illicit the proper reaction from my victims. These suckers were about to realize that they had just been...networked!

I worked the crowd and shook hands with the perfect business handshake. I know it was perfect because I was extremely successful with it. I have even taught other people how to use it. I looked at my watch and realized that I had put in my pre-decided thirty minutes. I gave my excuse to the person I was talking to and began heading for the door. About halfway there, I was stopped by a gentleman who reached out and put a business card in the lapel pocket of my suit coat. As he did, he said four words that I will never, ever forget....

You're doing it wrong.

He didn't even stop to talk to me. In fact, he didn't even miss a step in his stride. He never looked back, and he never paused to make sure I saw him. I know, because I watched him just disappeared into the crowd. I pulled out his card, and it was actually just a note.

It said:

See you Tuesday!

I had no idea who he was or what appointments I had on Tuesday, so I drove home and never thought about it again....

RIGHT!!!

I thought about it for the rest of the night. I thought about it as soon as I woke up the next morning. I couldn't wait to get to my office and see what I had on my calendar for Tuesday. I searched and searched and came up empty. The only person I had a meeting with on Tuesday was a long-term client, and I was pretty sure that she was not the gentleman from the museum. I had five days to figure it out.

Then I realized, "This is a trick." He is trying to get me to connect with him. He was networking me. I felt like Superman had just walked into a room full of Kryptonite. I was completely thrown off my

You're Doing It Wrong!

game. Now I was mad. "Nobody out-networks the Networking Man." I was not going to waste my time on him.

I tried to forget about him and just get back to my normal routine. I focused on my work and everything I had to do that day. I was not going to let him distract me even though he was so good at it: the way he approached me; the way he never looked back; the way he was just so able to...I was doing it. I was thinking about how he did it.

This went on for a very short time...okay, maybe a long time; actually, it went on until I climbed into bed Monday night. Tuesday morning, I jumped out of bed and couldn't wait to get to the office. I could not wait to see who was going to come see me that day. I had to meet this guy. I was so upset with him but at the same time I needed to get to know him. I needed to learn this ability to completely get into someone's head.

The day passed by as if in slow motion. I would sit in a meeting with someone, instantly disqualify them and be ready for the next meeting. All day and...nothing. I felt myself getting so upset. People in the office began asking me if I was okay.

"This guy has really gotten into my head," I thought.

At about 3:30, my boss called me into his office.

"Great. He probably noticed my mood."

I was going to have to reach deep into my bag of tricks and try to smile, laugh and assure him that I was fine and nothing was wrong.

"I need you to take my place at a dinner tonight. We are accepting a "Thank You" plaque for sponsoring a youth baseball team. You don't have to stay all night. I know you didn't plan on it, but make an appearance for me."

Whew! I wasn't in trouble.

"Sure, Sir. No problem."

I attended the event and shook hands, said my hellos and began my goodbyes. As I was headed to the door, there he was. Before I could even get close to him, I could tell he was speaking to me. I wasn't close enough to hear him, but I knew what he was saying.

You're still doing it wrong.

"What do you mean by that?" I asked.

He said, *Somebody went to the expense of throwing a party and you are just attending a networking event. In fact, you are being a party pooper.*

"Excuse me?" I questioned.

He continued, *I see so many of you young guys that are only here to get connections but you're missing the party.*

"It's my job, and I need those connections," I said.

Yeah, but you're not getting 'em. And none of these people want to meet with you again, do they? That's not networking, he said.

"Thank you, but I know how to network," I stated plainly.

~ 13 ~

No, you know how to collect business cards...and by the way, you really are good at that. If there was any value in it, you could really make your mark on this world. But if you want to really learn how to network and want to learn how to love doing it, follow me.

I followed him out to his car, and he didn't say a word the whole way there. When he reached his car door, he turned and said:

I didn't mean follow me to my car. I meant networking. 'Follow me networking.' You see, you are still wondering if there is something to this idea that you might be doing it wrong. You have a limited amount of success and are probably satisfied with the level of work you do for the return that you get. But you're curious. What if I'm right? What if things could be so much better? What if you could actually make an impact instead of just an impression? You are standing there thinking that you'll just find out as much information as you can and then decide. I understand

What if you could actually make an impact instead of just an impression?

that, but you are standing on the edge of a cliff, looking out at everything you could have and comparing it to everything you currently have. You are trying to evaluate whether or

~ 14 ~

not it is worth the effort. The problem is that you won't
actually know the rewards unless you jump...and that scares
you. What will it cost? What will I have to give up? How
much work? How much energy?

Well, I can tell you from somebody that has made the
jump...it's totally worth it. There is no reward without risk,
and this is a jump you want to make, but the choice is
yours...jump or stay.

Thursday, there's a party at Julio's. See you there.

I watched him drive away realizing that I didn't even
know his name. I returned inside and began asking everyone
I came in contact with about him. I eventually found out
that his name was John, and everybody loved him.
And thus began my education into the real world of
networking and my realization that I didn't know what I
was doing. I was ready to learn. I was ready to network. I
was ready to party.

R.S.V.P

Take a moment and evaluate your process of connecting with people.

Maybe it works well enough for you. Maybe you have a measure of success that you are comfortable with. Maybe you know deep down that while you may be impressing some people, you are not really impacting anyone. You are here at the edge of this cliff, and you get to decide to jump or stay. If you jump, everything changes: friends, family, workload, and even your free time.

If you stay, everything remains the same...you get to keep doing what you are doing. You get to keep wondering if there is a better way to connect with people.

Is that really what you want?

If you are making contacts but not really connecting, it may be time to start learning how to host your own party. Read on to find out more.

Hors d'oeuvres

Top of Mind

The number one reason customers give for contacting one company over another is not the internet, billboard ads or even the old phone book.

All of these contribute to name recall of companies, but customers' major reason for contacting a company is top of mind awareness.

On average, 63% of people requesting information from companies today will not be making a purchase for at least 3 months and another 20% will not be making a purchase for over a year.[1]

But when asked if they could recommend a contractor, a caterer, or a counselor; most people mentioned a friend they know, or someone they recently used.

They may see your billboard and they may "Like" your social media, but they will always remember you if you are friends.

Be "Top of Mind" with all your friends.

Let's Party!

It's My Party and...

Thursday came, and I realized that John was talking about the Chamber of Commerce After-Hours Networking Social at Julio's Cantina. I worked the crowd as usual and didn't see John at all...that is until the end of the evening when he walked through the door and everybody seemed to look his way and smile, almost as if they had been waiting for him to arrive.

He shook hands and smiled, just the way I do. He looked people in the eye and showed them respect by paying attention to them as they spoke, just the way I do. He made his way through the crowd as I just stood back and watched. We basically have the same technique.

He and I really didn't connect until we were getting ready to leave, but as we were walking out he asked me how my evening went.

"Great," I said.

How many business cards did you get? he asked.

~ 21 ~

"I'm not sure; about fourteen, I think."

That's too many, he said.

"How many did you get?" I asked.

Three, but one is a dud.

"So what, I should just throw these away?" I asked somewhat sarcastically.

He stopped walking and turned to me and said, *Any card in your hand right now that you can tell me the name and business without looking, you should keep. If you can't...throw it away.*

I couldn't actually remember a single name. I was flustered. I remembered a few businesses but not the name of the person for that business. But, isn't that what the card is for, so I wouldn't have to remember? There was no way I was going to throw away all of these great leads.

"I think we see things a little differently," I said.

Fine. Go add those to the pile on your desk from Tuesday. I'll see you at the luncheon on Monday and we'll try again.

And with that, he was gone.

As I sat in my office chair on Friday morning, I thought about the ridiculous idea of only collecting business cards from people I know. I pulled all of the cards I collected the night before out of my shirt pocket and placed them on the desk. As I began to organize them, I recalled the names of people who went with the companies.

Actually, I didn't recall them, I just read their names. I am not even sure I heard them say their names the first time. I stacked them up and sent out my usual emails to each of them.

Then and only then, did I add the business cards to my bottom drawer. It was full of them...people from all over with all kinds of backgrounds. I always save these cards in case I ever need to dig through and pull one out as a sale begins to appear. In actuality, I must admit that I have never had to go dig into my drawer and find their business card. Deep down, I think this drawer gives me validation for the work I do. I have proof that I met people, lots of people, pretty important people.

At the luncheon on Monday, I met some new faces. I couldn't help but try to remember their names and the names of their businesses. I wasn't going to be caught off guard again. I even looked over them as I ate lunch. I was totally ready. Then I saw John across the room. We met afterwards, and he asked me how many cards I collected.

"Nine," I said.

That's too many, he said once again.

"No, I know all their names and businesses," I stated proudly.

Tell me one.

"I met Stuart Johnson with Century 21 Realty," I said with great confidence. I was ready to go through the entire stack and tell him each and every name and business. This was so great. I'm sure John didn't realize what a quick learner I was. That was when the tough questions began.

How long has Stuart been there? Is he having a good year? What is the one thing Stuart needs right now? What color was his shirt? How long has he been coming to this luncheon? Can you tell me anything about Stuart?

"Uhh...."

I had nothing. I didn't know anything about Stuart. I didn't know anything about any of my contacts. I didn't know that was what I would be tested on. He continued.

You see, you are here to get something from these people. I'm not.

"Why are you here?" I asked.

It's my party, and I always attend my own party.

He left me sitting there thinking about what he said...not the party stuff, I had no idea what he meant by that. I was stuck thinking about the way I didn't know anything about Stuart's life. I remember talking to Stuart, but all I could recall was me trying to remember his name and business. I hated it, but he was so right. I was collecting business cards to further my sales. I know that

It's my party, and I always attend my own party!

~ 24 ~

sales and making money is not wrong, but I really wanted to learn to do it better and how to enjoy it more. I wanted people to look forward to me being there. I wanted people to call me instead of me calling them. I wanted to host my own party.

As he was walking away, I shouted, "How do I host my own party?"

Now you're getting it. Start with the location. We'll talk soon.

And he was gone.

Start with the location...what did that mean? Was he serious about me hosting a party?

R.S.V.P.

Take a moment and try to remember the last connection you made at a networking event, at church or even at work.

Do you remember anything deep about that person? Do you know anything about them that is worth knowing? You probably were not invited into their personal life at a very deep level, but that doesn't mean that you couldn't find something important about them.

Maybe a short email or text from you telling them that you enjoyed meeting them might help you dig a little deeper. This is not the usual business email that you probably already sent.

This would be a message saying simply,

You crossed my mind this morning, and I just wanted to say...I hope you have a great day!

When they answer the message you will find that you are in the middle of a conversation. Don't blow it by trying to tell them about what you are selling. Just talk, dig and listen for their answers. People love to talk about their favorite subject...themselves. Now...

Let's Party!

Hors d'oeuvres

Meaningful Communication

Customers do not regard your contacts with them for sales, orders, payments, appointments, service calls or even the obligatory Christmas cards as meaningful communication. These connection points only serve to help you after the relationship has been established as a friendship. Only then are you helping them because they are important to you. Otherwise, it is just part of your job.

Meaningful communication includes all the extra time and attention they receive from you without feeling like you are trying to close a deal. The more meaningful communication you have, the more trust is built and the more they become friends...and your friends will call you and recommend you to their other friends.

Location, Location, Location

I sat back in my office realizing that I could get much closer to my goals if I planned events and could motivate people to get there. Everybody would already know me, or know of me and want to be included in my party. This could be a real winner. Everybody loves to rub elbows with the host so I would be the important one. This could really be cool...but it could also blow up in my face. What if nobody comes? What if I invite everybody that I know and they don't remember me or worse, don't want to come because they are not impressed with me? What if they think this is just a way for me to capture more sales?

I determined to contact everyone in that drawer. I reached down and opened it. It was a large drawer designed to hold hanging files. Instead, it was holding about a thousand business cards. The good news was I had about a thousand people to contact and invite. The bad news was I had about a thousand business cards I needed to go through. I began pulling them out and laying them on the desktop. As I looked over all the different cards, I really began to dread this upcoming work. I spent most of the morning inputting all the invitees into a spreadsheet. Then I had a fantastic idea: I needed some help. Surely there was someone who I can pay to input all this data. So, after three and half hours of inputting names, numbers and addresses, I stopped. I put all of those business cards into a brown paper grocery sack and rolled the top of it, so they wouldn't fall out.

Impressive Number of Contacts

Later that week, I was having lunch with John at a little chicken sandwich restaurant called Chick-fil-A. He had called and said it was time to discuss the next step. As we sat there eating, I explained to him about all the cards that I had collected and my intention of paying someone to input them for me. I explained my plan to invite all of them and asked if he knew what kind of percentage of response I might get. Thinking that I would try to impress him with my contacts, I asked if he had ever held a party for a thousand people before. I casually followed that question up by asking if he thought a thousand was too many.

You're not even close.

"What, you mean it should be more?" I asked.

125,000 people

"Excuse me?" I asked.

You need to invite one hundred twenty-five thousand people to your party. These are real people; not contacts, not business cards, not names...people, real people.

I was stunned. That had to be for shock value only. There is no way you can host a party like that. I've never even heard of a party that big.

"How would I ever be able to afford that?" I asked.

You are getting way ahead of yourself here. The first thing we have to do is decide on a location.

"Okay. Where do I hold a party for 125,000 of my closest friends?" I asked trying to sound as sarcastic as possible.

You are misunderstanding what this party is supposed to look like.

He put down his fork, looked me straight in the eye and began teaching me about being a party animal.

Life Is A Party

Anytime, Anyplace...that is your when and where. You bring the party with you. You need to understand one thing...Life is a party. Just start celebrating and people will join in to be a part of it with you. When you celebrate life, you attract people around you who want to enjoy themselves and be in a better mood. You have been thinking

~ 33 ~

of the events that you go to as a way to make sales and find more people to put into the pipeline for future sales. I go to my events to bring life. I go to my events to bring the fun. I go to my events to bring the party...and people love it when I show up.

When was the last time somebody said, 'Oh good, the salesman is here?' You go to these events with sales as a cause. I go to these events and sales are the effect.

You attend these functions with sales as your goal. I attend these functions with relationships as my goal and sales are the result.

You go to these events with sales as a cause. I go to these events and sales are the effect.

When I host a party, I invite whomever I want; it takes place wherever I want; it happens whenever I want. I get to decide what we do; I even get to decide the whether it is going to be a great party or a bad party, and when the party is over. I am in total control of my party.

Work Your Way IN

But you need to understand something. People are not going to come to your party if you are not having fun. People are not going to come to your party if you are just going to ask them to buy something. People are not going to come to your party unless they know you, and they aren't going to know you until you know them. In order to really know them, you have to be in their lives; but if you don't genuinely care about them, they are not going to open up to you. They are going to resist you, so if you really want to know people, you have to learn how to work your way "IN."

> **INvite them**
> **INvolve them.**
> **INvest in them.**
> **before you can**
> **INvoice them.**

People don't mind paying for products or services. People don't even mind if you make money selling a product or a service to them. But people want to know that you care about the fact that they need your product or service. When you care about what others care about, what they care about will be you.

I know it sounds a bit cliché, but it's actually true. I have lived it, and now I love it. I have so many friends who buy from me because I am their friend, and that kind of customer is tough to pull away. I don't worry about my competition. My friends know that I am their friend even if they no longer do business with me; and that alone makes them want to do business with me.

When you care about what others care about, what they care about will be you.

You see, when your life becomes the party, it can happen anywhere. When you meet a friend for lunch, it's a party. When you see someone at the store, it's a party. When you are at church, it's a party. And when people see that you are bringing the party, the fun, the life...they will want to be invited. I have had people cross a crowded room full of people to get to me and ask me if they can use my service. That's when you know you are the party.

It's all about three things...Location, Location, Location. You need to be available Anytime, Anyplace; not available to sell, but available to care. The sales will take care of themselves. Any location you are in is a great location for a party. So bring the party everywhere you go.

By this time, he had finished his lunch. He stood up, took a last sip of iced tea and turned to walk away.

"So I should try to be nice and care about people?" I asked.

He stopped at the door of the restaurant, and I noticed that he had my bag of business cards. I didn't even see him pick them up off of the chair next to me. I watched as he opened the bag and dumped the whole thing into the waste basket that was right by the exit.

"Just focus on three things," he said. *"Location, Location, Location."*

My 25¢ Tip

I left there knowing exactly what I was going to do. This was fantastic. I could jump-start this new kind of networking today. I went to my office and checked in. As I walked around the office, I realized that I couldn't really network with any of these people. Because they are already in my business, there really was no use in connecting with them. Besides, they already knew me. So I signed out and decided to go to find some of my contacts.

I went to the grocery store. As I walked up and down the aisles, I saw plenty of people, but no one that I knew or had met before. Most of the people there would never be interested in the products that I have anyway.

I went to the hardware store...same scenario. The middle of the day was probably not the best time to go hunting for people that I knew at the store. They were all at their jobs.

Then I remembered what John said. "Bring the party." I realized that even though I didn't know any of these people, I was not bringing life into the situation anyway. What was my plan? Was I just going to turn on the smile and fun if I saw somebody I knew? I realized I had better practice being fun all the time.

Standing right there in the insulation aisle of this big box hardware store, I began smiling and saying "Hi" to people. I worked my way over to a guy who was loading a medium-sized package of insulation onto a cart. I reached up and helped him load it as I said, "Here, let me help you with that."

"Oh, I got it," he said, but I refused to let go until it was safely on his cart.

It only weighed about 15 pounds, but I was here to help and was ready to load his whole cart.

As I grabbed the second one off of the shelf, I asked, "How many are you getting?"

"Just one," he said as he began backing up and walking away.

A little old lady was standing right there and asked me to help her find a hinge for her antique trunk. I spent the rest of the day walking around the store looking for a hinge, SOS pads and a new plunger for her bathroom. She tipped me 25 cents.

I got home that night, sat in my chair in my living room and tried to think of all the locations to which I could bring a party; Chamber of Commerce, Economic Development Centers, church, softball games, just about everywhere. I came up with a great list of locations to host a party. I was actually beginning to understand what he meant. But I still had one problem...who do I meet with? John said it was 125,000 people, actual people. I don't even know 125,000 people. In fact, the people I know don't even know 125,000 people. How am I going to reach 125,000 people?

I called John and got his answering machine, so I left a message.

"John, I understand that the location of this party is everywhere. I understand that I bring the party with me; but if I have to do it like I did today, it is going to take me 125,000 days to meet people. Where do I find these people? You have to have some kind of system for finding people. Call me back."

I went to bed that night thinking of the real potential of 125,000 new contacts...I mean people, actual people.

R.S.V.P.

In what ways could you bring life to your next event?

Take a moment and think about the people you enjoy being around. What do they do that attracts people to them? Do they make you laugh? Is it because they are a comedian or just enjoying life?

Once there was a large manufacturing company rumored to be moving to our city. A friend of mine told everyone he came into contact with that they were definitely coming, but I was very skeptical. People loved to talk with him about it, but I was almost never asked my opinion on the topic. The company didn't end up coming, proving me right; but he had many more friends than I did. This led me to the realization that I can be right, but if I don't have any influence with people, it really doesn't matter.

Most of us want to be around fun, happy, positive-attitude people. If you become one of those life-giving people, you will attract others to you. We usually think of ourselves as positive people, until we actually evaluate.

Write down 10 things that you are negative or skeptical about. How can you see these things differently?

Write down 10 places to which you could bring the party. Now...

Hors d'oeuvres

Call a Friend

Studies reveal that 80% of all non-routine sales occur after at least five follow-up contacts.[1]

But...

    44% of sales people give up after the first rejection;

    22% give up after two;

    14% give up after three;

    12% give up after four.

Translation: 92% of all sales people give up before the fifth contact.

Nobody loves rejection, but if you use these points of contact to establish a relationship, then the five connections can be less stressful, more enjoyable and much more profitable.

Could it be that the only difference between the top 8% of all sales people and the other 92% is as simple as making friends?

Let's Party!

The Guest List

About a week later, John finally called me back. As I questioned him as to why he hadn't called me sooner, he said,

You don't need to rush this. You need to take time to really understand what we are doing here.

"Yeah, I know. I get it. Now I have some questions about these 125,000 contacts."

You're doing it wrong.

"What do you mean? I haven't done anything," I replied.

These aren't contacts.

"Sorry, I meant people," I stated, attempting to fix my error.

You're not understanding yet. I wanted you focused on Anyplace, Anytime and Bringing the party. You were not ready to focus on your guest list for the party. If you rush into this and skip an important piece of the plan, your party

is going to be a flop. I need you to realize the importance of what we are doing. You want to do this right, don't you?

"You're right, John, I do want to do this the right way. I want to be good at this. I want to view each and every one of my guests as people, not sales. So how do I get ready to understand the Guest List?"

Now you're getting it. Meet me at two at our usual place.

I'm not sure I can get away today. It's kind of a busy day here," I rebutted.

I'm sure you can work it out. See you at two.

...and the phone went dead.

I went into my boss' office and asked if he had a moment.

"I have an appointment at two o'clock today. I know we are busy with the...."

I didn't even finish my sentence before he said, "I'm sure we can handle it. Go ahead. Just make sure you make it worthwhile. You're still on the company dime."

"Yes sir, I will," I replied, somewhat shocked.

You Found Your Smile!

I was sitting at the Chick-fil-A restaurant where I met John the last time, and hoping that this was our "usual place." I had only met him here once before. The music playing in the background was soft and enjoyable. I wasn't sure if we were going to eat lunch or just have a meeting, but I had to have another one of those chicken sandwiches, so I went and ordered one. I thanked the smiling checkout girl as she handed me my receipt, and she replied, "My pleasure." I had really become hooked on this place.

I sat down and finished my late lunch, and as I looked up, I saw John walk in. He had an incredible smile on his face. It wasn't over-exaggerated, but it looked different. It was real. It was genuine. It was authentic. I truly believed he was looking forward to seeing me.

He sat down and said,

That's it. You got it.

"Got what?" I asked.

Your smile, your real smile.

"I was just noticing you smiling as you came through the door."

It's contagious. Makes you want to smile back, doesn't it?

"I guess it does," I said.

You can't fake this. People can tell the difference in caring or closing. They know if you are helping or hustling. They know if you are a friend or a fake. Be real. Always be real. You think you have to be "On" all the time. You think you cannot let people know that you are having a bad day. You're wrong. People don't expect you to be perfect. They don't even want you to be. They want you to be real, just like they are real. You cannot relate unless you are real.

"I see. I really do. So how do I be real with 125,000 actual people that I don't even know?" I asked.

Whoa! Slow down. You are not ready for 125,000 people. But you are ready to start. Take out a piece of paper and a pen. Write down 200 names of people who you know. These need to be people who you can call, and they would know who

People can tell the difference between caring and closing.

you are. I'm going to get more tea and say 'Hi' to Cheryl over there. Get started.

I pulled an old spiral-bound notebook out of my pack and began writing down the names of all the people I knew. I wrote like the wind. I wrote family, friends, neighbors, and people from church. I wrote names of leaders that I knew and even included everyone at work. I had over one hundred names...but that was it. I was empty. I couldn't think of any other people that I knew. I even included long-lost family from California. They wouldn't really remember me but one line about how we are related and they have to talk to me...right?

My Impressive List

After about 15 minutes, John was walking back to the table. He again had that great smile on his face.

"Good conversation with Cheryl?" I asked.

Great conversation; I connected her two weeks ago with a friend of mine who connected her with a friend of his. She just had her final interview this morning him and he called while I was talking to her. He offered her a position with his company. She is so thrilled!

"Wow! That's amazing," I said.

Actually, it happens all the time. Level Three Connectivity: it's the Three Circles of Networking.

"The three circles?" I inquired.

Well, let's not get ahead of ourselves. Let's start with your list. Have you got your 200 names?

"Only about a hundred, but they are good ones," I stated confidently.

I showed the list to John, and we sat there in silence as he perused it. I could tell he was very impressed. I might even get a pat on the back for this one. It may not have been two hundred names but I'm sure I did better than most people. After all, I'm no stranger to this networking thing.

Who are Gayle and Tommy Standler?

"They are my cousins."

When was the last time you spoke to them?

"...About a year ago, maybe a bit longer."

Cross them off, and cross anybody off the list who you have not spoken to in the last 3 months.

As I did what John told me to do, my list got shorter and shorter. I continued to cross people off the list until I was down to just 49 people. I was disappointed and confused.

"There is no way that normal people have lists with 200 names, and I can't even come up with 50," I said a little louder than needed out of frustration.

First of all, the fact that you call other people "normal" tells me that you may not be understanding our plan yet. Do you think you are better than these so-called "normal" people? Besides, who said it was a competition?

"Well, I just meant...."

You need to understand that you are normal. You are real. You are just like them. If you are better than them, you cannot connect and motivate them. They will always look at you as different, and therefore, what you do is not reproducible in them. You can strive to be the best version of yourself, but the competition is never with them. Your job as the host of the party is to make sure your guests all enjoy the party...each and every one of them. The party is for them, not for you. You are just the host.

"Yes, you're right. I just forgot."

Listen to me for a second. This is important. If you help people enjoy the party you are creating, you will enjoy it more...more than before, more than now and even more than your guests. There is a great fulfillment that comes from enriching other people's lives. Look at Cheryl over there. Do you think she will ever forget that I put her in touch with a friend and led her to her new job? Even after she has

The party is for them, not you. You are just the host.

moved on to another job, she will always remember me as a guy who helped her with no ulterior motives. She and her company will be my customers for years to come. But I didn't help her get a job to place her in a position so I could sell to her later. I did it for her. That's it.

"You're right, and I can see how much she truly respects you; but I only came up with 50 people," I said.

It's always 50. Everybody has 50 people that they know and can claim that actually know them. Most of us can only manage relationships with 50 people before something starts to fail.

"What about the 200 you asked me for?"

That was just to make you stretch, to make you think out of the box. But, you are missing the point...you have fifty fantastic people on that list.

~ 51 ~

"Well, 49," I said.

Well, you can add my name to that list. I'll be your number 50...but you are going to have to start caring about the things that I care about.

"I can do that," I stated.

My Core Network

This group of 50 people is your core network. So now, do everything you can to work your way 'IN' with these 50 people. Remember,

> ***INvite***
> ***INvolve***
> ***INvest***
> > ***before you can***
> ***INvoice.***

Now grab a new piece of paper and draw three columns on it.

"Are these the 'Levels of Connectivity' you mentioned?" I asked.

No, but what I'm about to show you will transform how you see people. This is how we classify all the people that we come into contact with. Some will be added to our 50 as others drop off, and some will never be added at all. Now label your columns A, B and C.

He continued teaching as I made my columns.

Everybody you come into contact with has the potential to enter into your core network. We break this network into three groups...A, B and C. When you first meet someone, you will begin to determine if they are going to be one of your 50. If they become one of your 50, they will fit into your C group to begin with.

Group C is made up of about 20% of your Core Network, or about 10 people. These are people who you are acquainted with and would like to get to know more. These people would probably be on your Christmas card list. It wouldn't be too awkward for you to go to dinner with these people. Sometimes people work their way into being a part of your network without your help. Maybe you run into them regularly and end up having a conversation with them. Maybe they strategically work their way in and you know them better than you expect. That is perfectly okay. Let them in. Your Core Network is going to be a very fluid group over the next few years.

Group B is made up of 60% of your Core Network, or about 30 people. These are people who you know well and know you pretty well. If someone from this group were in a bind, it would be understandable for them to ask to crash on your couch. People cannot infiltrate this group on their own. They have to be brought in by you. Only by you reaching out and strengthening the relationship can they be in Group B of your Core Network.

Group A is made up of the last 20% of your Core Network, or about 10 people. These are your family and closest friends. These people are the ones who you could call for anything; the ones who will always be there for you. Group A are the people that will sacrifice to help you succeed. The more you work your way "IN" to your Core Network, the more you will realize who your Group A members actually are.

I began relisting all the names in my Core Network into the columns that I had drawn. John paused for a moment while I was writing, but then he continued teaching.

The "C" to "B" Conversion

Your goal is to convert as many people from group C into Group B as you can while still managing all the relationship in your Core Network. Sometimes, just one more meeting or conversation will convert a person from Group C to Group B. The better you get at working your way "IN" to their lives, the more you will be able to manage Groups B and C. As you begin to Invite, Invest, and Involve these people, they will begin to work their way into your life as well. The more they work their way into your life, the easier it will be to manage these relationships. The easier these are to manage, the more people you will be able to have relationship with because it will come naturally to you. Do you understand what I am saying?

"Yes, I see it. If I will focus on being a friend, a real friend to people, then being a friend will come naturally to me, and therefore, be easier. Is that right?"

Exactly...and as people join Group B, they are much closer to you and much more available to help you grow your network. This makes using the Levels of Connectivity much easier. And with the Levels of Connectivity, you have access to the One Hundred and Twenty Five Thousand people that can change the world. Are you ready to see your levels?

As you begin to INvite, INvolve, and INvest in people, they will begin to work their way into your life.

"Yes...very ready," I said. "Let me guess: get out a sheet of paper, right?"

You got it. I want you to draw 3 circles, each one inside another. Then label the small one in the center "50" and the next outer one "2500" and then the last one "125,000." This is your network.

The Three Levels of Connectivity

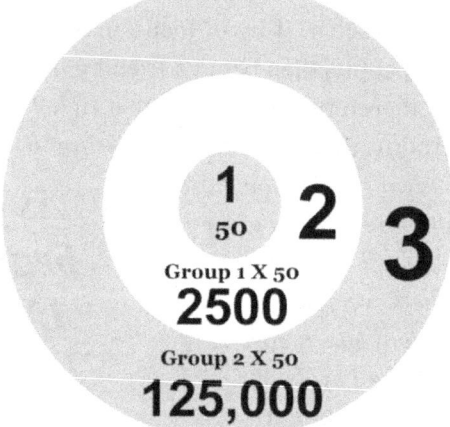

"Wait a second," I said. "I'm not understanding where you get those other numbers. Where did 2500 come from and how exactly did you get 125,000?"

Good questions. Let's look at it a little closer. You know 50 people, right? And as I told you, everybody knows 50 people who actually know them. So, your 50 people times the 50 people who they each know now puts you just one more step, or level, if you will, from 2500 people who would have a good reason to talk to you. After all, somebody who they know very well has introduced you. I don't know about

*you, but I would rather be introduced to somebody than to
meet them on a cold call.*

"Definitely," I chimed in.

*So on Level 1, you know 50 people. On Level 2, you
have access to 2500 people...."*

"...And on Level 3 we have..." I interrupted.

*Wait a second. I need you to think about this for a few
moments. In your line of work, would you be interested in
2500 names and numbers of potential buyers?*

"Yes, Of course I would. I would love 2500 good new
leads!"

*Well, think for a minute of having 2500 people that
want to meet you and possibly use your service because they
are a friend of yours.*

"You know, John, I have had all my insurance and
investments with the same company for years now, solely
because the representative is one of my best friends."

*Exactly, and I'll bet you have had other companies try
to get your business away from him, haven't you?*

"Yeah, I have. But you're right, there is no way I
would leave him. He does an excellent job and takes great
care of me."

*Now, think of having 2500 new friends who want to do
business with you because you do a great job; you take
great care of them and on top of all that...you are their
friend.*

~ 57 ~

"2500 new faithful customers would change my entire business!"

Now we are ready to talk about Level 3. Now you have 2500 friends, each one who would now like to introduce you to their 50 closest friends...that's 125,000 potential close friends. Your network of friends just exploded to a huge guest list for your party.

"That's fantastic! What a great source for business. First of all, I could use a whole lot more friends in my life. I love the idea of connecting with people that I would actually enjoy being around and would like to be around me."

And all they ask is one simple thing....

"To be treated like a friend, right?"

Actually, you are almost right. Remember, you have to be real. You have to be caring, not closing. You have to work you way "IN" and you cannot fake this. Sure, you can get away with faking it for a while, but as soon as you are found out, the whole system will collapse. You have to actually be a friend.

"You're right, I just misspoke. I plan on making more friends, and I would love to make friends with all of the people who are their friends.

I knew you understood. Take some time and just think about the different methods, techniques and steps to becoming a better friend, to your Core Network and to everyone else. We'll talk again soon.

I spent the rest of the day just dreaming about all the people who had things going on in their lives that I could actually care about. I pulled out a new piece of paper, listed each person in my Core Network, trying to write one important thing about their life and what they may be going through. It was much tougher than I expected. For many of the names on my list, I had no idea if anything had changed in the last 3-4 months. I made it my goal to find out something new about every one of these people. I had a huge job in front of me, and I wasn't going to make a dime doing it...but I was so excited about getting started.

R.S.V.P.

Write down the 50 people you know who actually know you.

Separate these into Groups A, B and C on an index card that you can carry with you.

Don't worry if the numbers you come up with are greater or less than 50 and don't be concerned if the ratios of the groups don't exactly match the suggestions of 20%, 60%, 20%. Your groups will be changing frequently.

Keep your list close as you concentrate on finding out important information about each person on the list. The more you connect with these people, the more you will learn about them, and the more you learn about them through personal connection, the more they will enjoy the fun, the life, the party that you bring.

Take one minute at the beginning of each day and read these names out loud to yourself. As you do, you will begin to remember things that you can ask each person about next time you connect.

Then, go ahead! Reach out and connect.

Now...

Let's Party!

50 People To
Work Your Way "In"

_____	_____
_____	_____
_____	_____
_____	_____
_____	_____
_____	_____
_____	_____
_____	_____
_____	_____
_____	_____
_____	_____
_____	_____
_____	_____
_____	_____
_____	_____
_____	_____
_____	_____
_____	_____
_____	_____
_____	_____
_____	_____
_____	_____
_____	_____
_____	_____
_____	_____

This is your core network!

Group A	Group B	Group C

Hors d'oeuvres

Play the Odds

"91% of clients say they are open to provide referrals. Yet, only 11% of salespeople ask for referrals." (Source: Dale Carnegie)[2]

"On average, referrals amount to 65% of a company's new business." (Source: New York Times)[2]

"84% of B2B decision makers begin the buying journey with a referral"(Source: Edelman Trust Barometer)[2]

"Referral leads convert 30% better than leads from other marketing channels." (Source: AMA Journal of Marketing)[2]

"Those that nurture leads make 50% more sales at a cost 33% lower than non-nurtured leads." (Source: Forrester Research)[2]

Most salespeople shy away from asking for referrals because:

a. Already got to "Yes"

b. Don't want to rock the boat

C. Don't want to be rejected.

Go ahead and rock the boat, Play the Odds, ask for referrals.

Let's Party!

Food and Entertainment

It had been a few days since I had spoken with John, but I was moving forward with the task of gathering information about the people in my life. As I did, I began to notice a few things about most of my friends. First, I realized that I have a lot in common with many of these people. There were so many of them that were at the same stage in life that I was as far as marriage, children and even age range. This made it incredibly easier to plan connection times that would work for both of us. The second thing that I realized was that most of these people had real situations that needed to be known. Some of them had sicknesses in the family; some of them were contemplating moving or changing jobs. But all of them just needed someone to know about their life and be a friend. More and more I found myself able to be that friend.

I was sitting at my desk on Tuesday morning when John called and suggested we get together and talk.

"Great! I have a ton of questions like, 'How do I get my friends to introduce me to their friends?' I hope you have a ton of answers."

Whoa, slow down. We have got a lot of planning to do before we get there. Meet me an hour before the Women's Luncheon tomorrow in the lobby at the Hilton and we'll talk a bit more.

"The Women's Luncheon...?" I questioned. "Why are you going to that?"

We...you mean, why are we going to that? I bought you a ticket too. We'll be the only two guys in the room. Tell me you don't want to go to a party full of women.

"Uhh...I guess so," I said.

See you there an hour early.

...and the phone went dead.

I spent the rest of Tuesday trying to concentrate on work, but I couldn't help but think about how awkward it was going to be attending a women's luncheon. I felt like John was asking me to rifle through a lady's purse. There are some things that you just don't do. Some things are just sacred. Are women's luncheons one of those things? Do I even want to know the things that they are going to be talking about? And most of all...are they going to be upset that two men are there? I don't need a bunch of women mad at me and my company.

John and I met in the lobby of the Hilton on Wednesday at 10am. I was there by 9:20 hoping that if I got there early enough, no one would think that I was here for the estrogen-powered, feminine tea party. I went to the restaurant and ordered a black coffee. The server asked me if I needed cream.

"No. I like it black...and strong," I instantly answered feeling the need to express my masculinity.

She returned a few moments later with a simple cup of coffee. After one sip, I wanted some cream so badly, but there was no way I was going to ask for it.

John arrived and sat down across from me.

Are we ready to plan the food and entertainment?

"Wait, why are we really here?" I questioned.

What do you mean?

"Why are we coming to a Women's Luncheon? Wait, are you the guest speaker?"

No. The speaker is a lady who wrote a book about how to succeed in business.

"...as a woman. You mean, how to succeed in business as a woman, right?"

Yeah, as a woman.

"Again, why are we here?" I questioned.

Well, I'm here to host a party. Why are you here?

"I'm here because you told me to be here, but I feel kind of out of place," I said.

Just relax. You are hosting this party as well, and you need to learn to enjoy your own parties. Don't over-think this. That look you have on your face right now is similar to the look you had when we first met. You didn't want to be there, and I saw it all over you from across the room. Believe me, if you don't want to be

I'm here to host a party. Why are you here?

here, these women don't want you here. But if you can bring life to this party, they will invite you back every time they get together. I don't force my way into their meetings; they invite me. I respectfully asked them if I could invite somebody that I thought they needed to have at their meeting, and they said I could. Now, they are not looking to open this up to men, but they are expecting you to bring value to what they are already doing, so you are going to have to prove yourself. You have to go in there and bring life and fun to this party. You have to go in there and take control and make this party yours. If you can't do that, they are never going to invite you back. Are you understanding what I mean?

Yes, I am...but what do I have to bring to a women's meeting that they don't already have?" I asked.

They don't have a man that is willing see things from their point of view and try to help them achieve their goals. They don't have a man who is willing to come to a room full of women and listen, and empathize and learn what they want out of life. This is the perfect place for you to begin stretching your networking muscles and meet some new friends.

"But what does this have to do with my Core Network?" I asked.

Everything...this has everything to do with your Core Network. You need to realize that your life should be made up of a series of instances in which you connected somebody to a friend of yours, or you created a relationship for a friend of yours to a new connection you just made. I can almost guarantee that someone in that room upstairs will need something that one of your friends provides, not just in business but in life. If you make that connection possible, they will never forget it. If you connect 3, 4 or5, they will appreciate you being here. If they really appreciate you being here, they will let the leadership know, and the leadership will invite you back. Some of the ladies in that room are my customers. Some of them are just friends. They all try hard to introduce me to the new people who are here today because they want others to benefit from being my friend. You see, most people in this world are good, honest people who actually want to help others. I just give them an easy way to feel like they are a part of something great. They know that I am going to treat their friends the same great way that I treat them, and that excites them. When I connect their friend with the right person who will further their career, or be their family doctor, or even become their best friend, they will always remember who introduced them. That makes them part of a great life story. It gives them a

It gives them a legacy... something in their life that they can point to and feel good about.

legacy...something in their life that they can point to and feel good about. And that is more powerful than any sales pitch I could ever write.

"Wow! I get it. I felt like I was here to crash their party, but I am actually here to serve. I'm here to make sure that all of these wonderful people have everything they need and have a wonderful time at this party. I'm here to host. I get it!"

Now you're seeing it. Think you can do that today?"

"I know I can. You know, just when I think I have this networking thing figured out, you add another dimension to it."

Yup, and we have a lot more to do, so let's get started. You need to understand that this is a lifestyle, not a job. You have a job, and this is not meant to replace what you are doing. The work you are doing for your company is important and actually needed for the company and for you. What I am teaching you is not going to happen overnight. You have to allow yourself and your network time to realize who you are and why you do what you do. It is very important to not forget the job you have been hired to do.

You have a job to find new customers, pre-qualify them, approach them, meet with them and present your company to them, resolve their issues, close the deal and eventually follow up with them. You cannot neglect this. But you can now begin to do this with a

You cannot help people if they don't know what you have to offer.

foundation of networking that will add value to your friend's lives. There is nothing wrong with letting people know what you do for a living.

"So how do I incorporate networking into the job I am currently doing?" I asked.

First of all, don't go anywhere without a business card. I have acquired so many customers by offering my business card simply as a friend. I tell people to call me and we'll get together for a cup of coffee. I know they are never going to call, but I just got my business card in their hands. I always make sure they know what I do for my company, and I always let them know that I am here to help.

"I have a great 30-second pitch that I use to tell people about my products," I said.

That's fantastic! We're going to change it.

"No really, I have a great pitch," I stated.

Nobody wants to hear about your product in 30 seconds. You probably give it at every networking breakfast you go to. You stand up and tell a room full of people what you do and how great you do it in 30 seconds and then listen to them give their 30-second pitch. Have you ever made a sale that way?

"Yeah, I think I have?" I said confidently.

Really...after hearing about you, your company and your product for less than 30 seconds, somebody came up to you and handed you money for your product?

"Well, no...not quite like that."

You need a 30-second talk, but it should be designed to make people want to talk to you. Nobody is going to run up to you just because you say, "I sell widgets and you should buy one." You need to create a situation in which they need to find out more from you."

"Like what?" I asked.

I always bring a door prize to donate at meetings; but the door prize always brings people to me.

"You mean like your business card inside?" I asked.

If you got a bottle of wine with a business card attached to it, would you go out of your way to contact that person?

"Sure."

Really?

"Okay, probably not. So what do you donate?"

Our CEO wrote a great book. I make sure it's known that I will get her to sign it for the winner. Sometimes they announce it when they award the prize but I always put a note inside the first page.

You need to create a situation in which they need to find out more from you.

"That seems like a difficult process...to introduce a random person to your CEO every time you give away a book," I said.

Oh, I just make the offer for her signature and they come ask me how. I offer to take the book and get her to sign it. Then, I take it to them when we meet for coffee. I have never had anyone complain that I didn't bring my

CEO to coffee with me. I'm not sure they expect me to be able to do that, but they are always grateful for the effort I take to get them a signature from the CEO of our great company. And our CEO is actually pleased to sign her books for fans. After all, one of the great things about being an author is finding out that people really appreciate what you write and want you to sign your autograph personally to them.

"That's a great idea," I said. "But my CEO didn't write a book. Besides, that book just came out last year. What did you do before that?"

I would give gift certificates for services like massages, pedicures, golf lessons and just about anything else that gets me to my goal...and I always include a note that says contact me for details.

"But how does a gift certificate for a massage make somebody want to come meet you?"

...because the person I bought the gift certificate from is one of my friends. Actually, they are in my core network. They know me and they know that I am reaching out to the person who is coming in to their business with this gift certificate. So, while they are trying to perform a great service in order to win a long-term massage customer, they are also going to be talking about how I have helped them. I will be the topic of conversation. In fact, I make sure of it when I buy the gift certificate. They even give me a discount

because they know that I will be highly recommending them. Even after the service, when I get together with the winner, I will be discussing how much I really like my friend and their business, further establishing the winner as a customer of theirs.

"That sounds like a lot of selling for a system that isn't supposed to involve selling," I said.

Let me ask you this. Did you like your lunch the other day at Chick-fil-A?

"Yes, I actually did."

"Have you been back there without me?"

"I've actually been back twice. Why?"

...because, the owner of that franchise is a friend of mine. His name is Scott, and I helped him find and buy that business. I meet people there all the time. I know that he is going to do a great job with the meal. I know that the service is going to be great and I know that the place is going to be clean. He will have music that I like playing and will always make my other friends comfortable. Now, do you feel like I was selling to you there?

"No, I didn't even know that you knew the owner."

Right, but you liked his business and are now a customer of his. Are you mad at him for charging you for his service?

"No, not at all."

Of course you're not. You are willing to pay for that service and even appreciate the great job he does. This is how it is when you do a good job for your friends. Your friends appreciate the job you do and want to patronize your business because it is a great product, you have great service and most of all, they like you. They know that if they put their friends in contact with you and your business, that you are going to take care of them. That is real networking...networking as a lifestyle. Don't be afraid to tell people what you do. Don't be afraid to tell people about your products and service. People actually want to know. If you are proud of what you do, let everybody know. If you are not proud of what you do, then you need to find something else to do.

Don't be afraid to tell people about your products and service. People actually want to know.

Everything you do in life is an opportunity to connect somebody you know to somebody else you know; and if you do it correctly, they will always remember and appreciate it. They will want to connect you with everyone they know because it is a natural reciprocation. As you appreciate their connections, your friends will connect you more and more. Do you remember Cheryl?

"Yeah, the lady that you met...wait a second. You saw her here."

Of course. Did you think that was coincidence?

"Yeah, I actually did," I said.

She has become one of Scott's friends as well. She called me yesterday and told me that her boss was discussing their vendor contract and that she suggested that they shop around. Her boss agreed and next thing you know, I am having a meeting with him on Friday morning.

"That's great. So this is just a straight sales meeting? Now I see how this comes full-circle, back to selling," I said.

Nope. You're doing it wrong again.

"Okay, what am I missing?"

Remember how Cheryl got that job?

"Yeah, it was a friend of yours."

Would you rather sell to a cold call or a friend of a friend?

"A friend...I get it. Your going to have your friend meet you on Friday morning, aren't you?"

Actually, he set up the meeting. Now I have Cheryl on my side with her influence, and Tom, my other friend, arranged the introduction over breakfast. What do you want to bet that I walk out of there with a contract for our service?

"Uhh...no, thank you. I'm sure you will."

You see, networking isn't just about what you can get and what you need to accomplish. It's about being a part of a group, a family, a network. You are just one member of the team and your team can all prosper if you all work together. You can be such a huge benefit to so many on your team who would love to be a benefit to you, but you need to find out as much as you can about them and let them know all about you. It is perfectly fine to tell people what you do. In fact, it is necessary.

Meet with as many people as you can and use every single time, connection and point of interest to further something for one of your other contacts. The more your network is tied together, the stronger it is. The stronger you network is, the more your entire team prospers.

The stronger you network is, the more your entire team prospers.

"Wow. I have never considered that it could go this deep."

As Zig Ziglar said, "You can have everything in life you want, if you will just help other people get what they want."

"I have always loved that quote but never really knew what it meant until now. I get it. I really get it. It is all coming together now. But let me ask you a question: Is there any way to accelerate these connections? I don't want to short circuit the system, but there has to be a way to let my friends know that I want them to introduce me to their friends."

There sure is, but it is not a shortcut. It is just a different way of getting to the same point. This is a fantastic step that you can take with your friends. Some will have an answer right away, and others will have to think about it for a while. There is a question that you can ask each one of them that will get you where you want to go. But before you do, you have to make sure you have laid all the groundwork. You have to have proven yourself to them and earned their trust. The more network contacts you have expressing your talents and integrity to them, the easier it is going to be to get their trust. Sometimes you just have to put in the time and create that trust from scratch, but you have to get it. If you don't have their trust, you will get a corrupted answer and be led down the wrong path. It is just a bad as collecting business cards from everyone and not getting anywhere with trying to sell to them. Getting an

*answer to this question without earning their trust will just
cause a lot of extra work for a very low return.*

"Okay, so what is the one question?" I asked.

He sat back in his chair and looked at me, making sure
I was ready. Then he calmly changed his tone from a
teaching position to a very friendly composure.

Who do you know that you think I should meet?

As I sat and thought about that question, I realized that
he was so right. What a great question...but what a huge
diversion if I didn't have their
trust. People would be
introducing me to people who
they don't really have any
standing with. They would
just be recommending me to
people in general because they
don't really know me. I would

*Who do you
know that
you think I
should
meet?*

be just one of the people they have met. But, if I have their
trust, then they would actually want me to meet their close
friends. In fact, they would want me to do business with
their close friends. I must have had some strange grin on my
face because I noticed John just sitting there watching me,
and he was beginning to smile.

You get it don't you?

"Yeah, I get it," I said. "That's fantastic...and because it will go completely wrong if I don't earn their trust, it keeps me from asking it to everybody just for the sake of trying to build a bigger business. I have to do it right. I have to absolutely do it right. No short cuts. I love it!"

John stood up to leave.

"Wait, I'm not finished. I have a lot more to talk about."

Later; we have a meeting to get to. Are you ready for this?

"When I got here this morning, I thought I might find a way to get out of going to this Women's Luncheon. But now I want to go to it. I am actually looking forward to it." *Just wait until the next one when they ware looking forward to you coming to their meeting. That's when it really gets fun.*

R.S.V.P.

Do you know someone in your Core Network who needs to meet someone else in your Core Network?

Do you know someone in your Core Network who needs you to be a friend today by sending them an encouraging text, email or even a hand-written note?

Do you know someone in your Core Network who you have built up trust with and are now at the point in which you can ask them, "Who do you know that you think I should meet?"

Begin building trust with all of your Core Network by encouraging, contacting and simply, by being available to listen.

Remember----Work your way "IN"
INvite
INvolve
INvest in them

Build trust in your Core Network, and you will find that they will not only ask you for your product or service, but they will also recommend your service to everyone they know. Then you can INvoice them without regret. Now...

Let's Party!

Hors d'oeuvres

Email

A study of over 5 million emails revealed why you may not be getting the return rate you would like:[3]

- The average person deletes 48% of all emails they receive.

- Using all caps in the subject line hurts response rates by close to 30%.

- Subject lines with 3 to 4 words get more responses than shorter or longer ones.

- Messages written at a third-grade reading level are 36% more likely to get a reply than those written at the college reading level.

- The more you write, the less likely you are to get a response.

Use email to strengthen the relationship already established with your friends and avoid attempts to use it to close a sale. Be a friend and get a reply instead of getting deleted.

Let's Party!

Clean Up

The Women's Luncheon was amazing. John was a hit with his smile and genuine, caring attitude. I tried to emulate what he did or what I thought he would do in every situation. I paid attention when one of the ladies told me about her business, and I actually thought of a member of my Core Network who would love to meet her. As I was telling her about my friend, I watched as her expression changed. I could actually see in her face the appreciation that she was feeling for connecting her. I thought to myself that I had better not drop the ball on this...but I really didn't think it would be a problem this time. I genuinely wanted to connect these two ladies and it had nothing to do with me making a sale or getting a new customer of my own. I really wanted this lady to meet my friend for her good.

The more I contemplated the way I was feeling, the more overwhelmed I was by the success of true networking.

I was really hooked. It was so much fun and I could see myself doing this for the rest of my life.

I met so many other people at the luncheon, and many of them got a real kick out of the fact that John and I were interested in coming to their meeting. I left there with a handful of business cards from ladies who I had spoken with. I thought about the number of cards that were in my hand and actually had no idea how many there might be. But I did remember every conversation I had. It was as if I was having lunch with long-time friends. The thought of selling to them was not even on my mind.

About a week later, I was sitting at my desk when the phone rang.

Hey, bud. Are you ready to learn the next step?

"The next step...? How many steps are there?"

Technically, they are infinite, but for our purposes, there is just one more. Meet me at two at Chick-fil-A.

"Wait, not today. I really can't. My boss will never agree to me leaving today. We have a full staff meeting from one to three."

Yes, he will. See you at two.

"No, I really...." and the line went dead.

I sat there stunned. I really appreciated all that John has invested in me and I really appreciated his friendship as well; but there was no way I was going to ask my boss for the afternoon off to go sit at Chick-fil-A and talk about networking. He wants sales; he wants customers, and we were about to have a required meeting to talk about just that.

About 12:30, I was headed to the conference room to set my notebook and pen down at a specified seat. I knew for a fact that my boss has a tendency to favor people on his right. I wasn't sure exactly why, but he does and I was definitely going to take advantage of it. As I was walking into the conference room, I heard a voice behind me calling my name. It was my boss.

He said, "I heard you have an appointment at two. Have a good meeting and let me know how it goes."

"Uhh...okay sir. I will."

I had no idea what just happened but I was definitely going to get out of there before he changes his mind or I get noticed by somebody else in the office and this blows up into an issue that I have to explain. I left and went to grab lunch at Chick-fil-A. I sat there just watching the action in the restaurant. I noticed a gentleman who seemed to be in charge. Not because he was barking orders, but because all of the employees seemed to be very respectful to him. They were still laughing and smiling but something just said that he was the boss. He grabbed a towel, and headed out to the dining room and began to wipe down tables as he said hello to some of the customers. As he approached me, he asked if I enjoyed my lunch.

"Yes, I really did...and you have a great restaurant here."

"Thank you. My name is Scott, and if you need anything, you just let me know."

"I sure will Scott, and my name is Brad...great to meet you."

Just then John came through the door. Before Scott turned away I said, "Hey Scott, I need something."

"What can I get for you?" he asked.

"Whatever this gentleman buys, I'll cover it, okay?" I asked.

"You bet," he whispered as he turned to see John coming up behind him.

I see you met my friend.

Scott and I answered in unison, "I sure did."

John and Scott visited for a while, and then John sat down at my table.

"I thought we were meeting at two," I said.

We are. I just came in for lunch. But since we are both here....

Conversation began as we were both eating. I couldn't stop talking. I was telling him everything from how much I enjoyed the Women's Luncheon to how I connected a lady there to someone in my Core Network. Then came the question I could not get out of my mind:

"Did you call my boss and tell him I had a meeting at two?"

Of course, this is important.

"...and he just agreed? Just like that...?" I asked.

I've been trying to tell you...when your friends know you and trust you; they are willing to give you what you need.

"Wait...you know my boss?"

I've known Steve for years. The first time I saw you was the night that he called me and asked me to reach out to you. He said that I have carte blanche and has paid for all the lunches and events that we have been attending. He has even been calling me to ask about your progress. He really believes in you and wants you to succeed.

"Are you kidding me? I didn't think he liked me very much. I thought all he cared about was sales."

No. You really don't know him at all. He built that entire company by networking. I have watched him build his entire business through relationships. Steve is one of my Core.

This world always remembers significant people.

"So he's paying you to teach me?"

No...I am doing this because I believe in it, and I believe in you too. You have a desire to really help people.

That is something I love to feed. You can survive this life and get to the end, or you can find a way to be successful. You...have found a way to be successful at what you do. But the world doesn't remember successful people for very long. However, if you find a way to impact other people's lives...then you become significant. This world always remembers significant people. Now, you have found a path to being significant in people's lives.

"You're right. I have had a great week. I feel like I have found my calling in life. I could see myself networking for the rest of my life."

Well then, we had better learn the last step. This is probably the most important step in the process. Unfortunately, it is the one thing that most of us leave incomplete. Do you know what they call the forth batter in the lineup of a baseball team?

"Uhh, yeah. Clean up."

Right. You know why?

"Well, because he has the job of finishing strong and bringing the batters on base all the way home," I said.

Right, and that's what we do now...clean up. You have to make sure everything you have done up to this point is completely accomplished, not in your mind, but in the mind of your friends. This is where we make sure that we have delivered more than we promised. Look at Scott over there.

As I turned, I saw the owner of the restaurant wiping down a table over by the window.

Nobody has sat at that table since I have been sitting here, and yet he is still out here wiping it off and making sure that the flower in the vase and the table tent is perfectly placed. Now my lunch is going to taste the same whether that table is clean or dirty. But Scott has learned that he is not just serving food, he is serving an entire experience. He is going to make sure that everything under his control is going to be perfect for me while I am at his establishment. And not only is he sending a subtle message to me, but he is also showing every one of his employees to operate the way that he does. With his leadership, this place is always clean, always smells fresh, and is always welcoming when I come in. However, the menu boards over the register do not say anything about the tables being clean. They don't say that all the staff here will smile and be happy to serve you. All of the things that are done without being advertised or agreed to are completely extra...but it is those little things that keep me coming back. Most of the time, I don't even notice all the extras I get with my meal.

"I get it...under-promise and over-deliver. But what if I promised too much at the beginning? What if I over-promised?"

There is no such thing as an "over-promise!"

"What do you mean? Of course there is."

There is no such thing as an under-promise and there is no such thing as an over-promise. If you promise me something, it's just that...a promise. It's not an under-promise and it's not an over-promise. We like to call it an over-promise because it tends to spread out our poor customer service over a

There is no such thing as an "over-promise!"

number of issues and maybe even over a number of different employees. But we only seem to determine it to be an over-promise based on our ability to deliver. The real truth of the matter is that you made a promise, now what are you going to do about fulfilling it?

So you have a choice to make. You can either determine to over-deliver on that promise or you can choose to lose that customer, that client, that friend and just under-deliver. And then you can hope that friend will never talk to any of your other friends about how disappointed they were with you and your service. And then you can also hope that you never do that again because you can only host so many bad parties before people stop showing up to them.

By the way, in case it is not obvious...the first choice is the right one.

"Right, I'm sure it is. But you're saying that I can have a few mistakes and still have great success...right?" I suggested.

Yes, but your goal is not to be successful. Your goal is to be significant.

You might make a mistake and promise something you cannot fulfill, but that mistake can be fixed by finding a way to fulfill it and then doing more. Over-delivering will always fix a mistake like that, but under-delivering is a choice, not a mistake.

"What do you mean? Why can't under-delivering be a mistake too?" I asked.

Because if you make a promise, there is nothing you can do to go back and change that. You have given your word, and it is not changeable...it is what you said. You may try to change the agreement you have or the promise you made, but you can never remove it from happening.

Your integrity is shown to be strong or weak in your delivery.

Delivery, on the other hand, is something you can always adjust. If you have under-delivered, just deliver more...problem solved.

Your promise is not your integrity; it is an opportunity for your integrity to be seen. Your integrity is shown to be strong or weak in your delivery. If you do more than you say you will, your integrity will be seen as strong. You will gain a reputation for being a person everyone will want to be around because they know exactly where they stand with you. If you under-deliver, however, your integrity will be shown to be weak, and people will tolerate you as long as they have to...and then they won't.

"What if I can't deliver what I promised?" I asked.

Well, you will learn to not make promises that you cannot keep, but you can always find a way to try to make things right with your friends. Find something that is not on "Your Menu" that you can give to or do for your friends each and every time. There is always something that you can give to your friends that they are not expecting. There is always one more way that you can make an impact.

"Oh, I get it... promise, and over deliver. That makes total sense," I said.

A good friend of mine has a plumbing company. He instructs every one of his employees to find one extra thing that they can do for each and every customer they service. They always add it to the invoice with a charge of $0.00. This tells the customer that they received more service than they paid for. This is one of the reasons that his customer service surveys end up with a 99% approval rating.

"That's fantastic. I love that idea! I'm going to implement something like that into my relationships with all of my friends," I said.

Great, but before you do that, let's start by covering all the bases. There are a number of steps that will help you be significant in people's lives.

How to End the Party

First, you have to know how to end a party. Ending a party is just as important as starting a party. You have to respect your friend's time. Every single person on this earth has the same number of minutes in the day, and many of them are very particular about how they spend those minutes. You have to respect them enough to allow them to decide how many of those minutes they are willing to give you. When you set up a meeting with a new friend, take up a shorter period of time...so many of us rage against this step. We think that if we can make a sale, then we should. We think that if we can take a few more minutes, then we should. We fear that we may not get another chance.

However, we are growing relationships here, not sales. You may get a sale today, but each sale will be evaluated based on numerous points such as need, salesmanship, sales resistance, quality of the service, and even the feeling that they have after the sale. If any one of these areas is sub-par, good luck getting a repeat sale. And remember, as the point man on the account, you are not really in control of all aspects of your companies connection with each client, but you are the one that they think about when they think of your company. Any poor performance on the part of your company or any weak link in the company will be attributed to you...and without a relationship, they will not even bother telling you why they won't do business with you anymore.

But...take time to establish that relationship and everything changes. When things go wrong, you are the one your friend will call, and you have the opportunity to make things better, and in turn, strengthening the relationship. Your sales and your repeat sales are much more in your control.

Take time to establish that relationship and everything changes.

As you get to know people more, you can take more time, but you will learn to watch their body language. You'll know when your time is up. You always want to end the party before they tell you it's over. Then, you can always invite them to your next party.

Always Leave Them Wanting More."

"So are you really saying that I shouldn't sell to somebody until the third or forth visit? That seems really odd. I'm not sure I could walk away from a sale just because we just met," I said.

No; not completely. There are definitely times that you can and should sell product or service to a customer. You have a job to do, and you need to have integrity with your company as well as with your customer. However, you are not just selling a product. You are selling your company.

If you asked owners of companies it they would rather have their customers think of them as friends or a businesses, I would bet they would all answer in unison, "Friends."

If you have the chance for a sale, you should take it, unless it compromises your position as a friend. Your company has to continue to make sales year after year or it will cease to exist.

One of the best ways to be able to revisit a friend is to leave them wanting more. Think about the gatherings you have had with friends that you wish had lasted a little longer. I have had so many of them: lunches with amazing people, evening dinners with good people who I would like to know more, and even great vacations. Sometimes I wish my vacations would last forever. But the reason I feel that way is because I left there before I was done. If I had left there after I was completely satisfied, I would have no reason to go back. We return to those situations to glean more experience, more fun, and more enjoyment; and that's how you need to leave all of your friends feeling. If they have an excellent experience and want it to continue, they will be at your next party.

Always Follow Up

"So I end the meeting...sorry; I end the party on my terms so that I can have another one. And I always leave my friends wanting to see me again. I get it. It actually makes sense and seems like it should be obvious."

Yes, but we always seem to revert back to the quick meeting. It really seems to be so much easier to just make a sale and move on. But if you will dedicate yourself to helping others get what they want, you can....

"...have whatever I want," I finished.

That is exactly right. But the next thing you need to remember is to always follow up. It seems pretty straight forward and yet it really is not. It is sometimes difficult to follow up when you didn't sell anything, didn't try to sell anything and didn't even talk about selling anything. Now you have to follow up just to say "Hi."

You can follow up by email or by text and make a good impression, but one of the best ways to further make an impact is to write things down. A simple "thank you" card can be a huge step towards helping someone remember you, and it is a great way to begin INvesting in them. When you take the time to write someone a hand-written letter or card, it says that you value them. This simple little gesture could have lasting effects on your relationship in the future. Send out thank you cards; add them to your holiday card list, and of course include them in your regular emails and text messages. All of these things work together to strengthen their belief in you as a friend; not just a salesman that they do business with from time to time.

The Invoice

"So I guess the initial contact with my future friends could be considered the INvite; the meeting could be considered the INvolve and the follow-up could be the INvest." I stated.

"That's one way to look at it, but don't ever forget that working your way IN is not a checklist to mark off in an attempt to get to the INvoice. If you have that attitude, your customers will see it and know that you are only fulfilling a quota and don't really have their best interest at heart. If you have not truly invited them into your life, and have not truly involved them in the party, and you have not truly invested in them, then you will be on shaky ground when you go to invoice them.

Understand that invoicing your friend is not just about making a sale. It is not just about getting money from your clients. It is about so much more than that.

When you ask a friend for a favor, you are invoicing. When you sell to a friend, you are invoicing. When you make a mistake and need time to correct it and even have to change the agreement, you are invoicing. Anything that you ask someone for is an invoice.

Even when you are just asking for 15 minutes of someone's time, you are invoicing.

Anything that you ask somebody for is an invoice.

Think about it this way: everything you do for someone else is like depositing capital into a relationship account. Every time you ask something of that person, you are making a withdrawal on that account. Your first meeting from a cold call is often operated on credit because you haven't deposited anything into that account yet. If the meeting goes well and everything from your personality to your promise of service operates together, you may get back to even in the account. If it goes really well, you may have a positive balance in that account that you can draw from later without getting into the negative. But if it goes poorly, you will stay in the negative and probably not get a second meeting, because this person already extended credit to you and in their mind, you did not repay.

The more deposits you have into this account, the more withdrawals you can make without putting the account at

~ 104 ~

risk. Some things that you do will be a huge deposit such as connecting them with a friend of yours who ends up being a big customer for them. Some things will be very small deposits such as a thank you email or text. But anything you do that benefits them is a deposit into that account.

If you really want what some companies call "Raving Fans," then just continue to make deposits into all of your friends' lives and the INvoicing will take care of itself. Always make sure you have more in your account than you are ever withdrawing.

"Wow! That makes a lot of sense. If I just take care of my friends, they will take care of me," I said.

John stood up and started heading out.

"When are we meeting next?" I asked.

"That depends on how you decide to follow up...this was your party. Remember, I'm now part of your Core Network and I must say that I have enjoyed the party so far...and thanks for lunch.

With that, he was gone, and I realized that I was officially into the party-planning stage of my life. The more I partied, the more I found people that wanted to party. The more I hosted, the more I discovered that a party is the best time to do just about anything: business, communication, friendship, caring, giving...everything was done better during a party. I had found my calling in life. I was a party animal.

R.S.V.P.

Think of the people in your Core Network who you may have been INvoicing without realizing it. Are there people in your network who you are operating on relationship credit?

Make a list of ways to begin making deposits into each account. The more deposits you have, the sooner you can get back to even in each account and eventually get ahead. Staying in the positive in each relationship places you in a great position to be a great friend...and people love having great friends.

Remember...Work your way "IN"
INvite
INvolve
INvest in them

Make continual deposits, big or small, into your Core Network, and you will end up with a huge community of friends who are willing to be there for you just as you have always been there for them. Then INvoicing them becomes just part of the friendship. Now...

Hors d'oeuvres

Rejection Desensitization

Simply put...get used to "NO."

Up to 98% of all sales are rejected on the first sales call.[1]

A guitarist's fingers hurt initially, so he works to build up calluses on them.

A weightlifter increases his overall strength by progressively adding resistance.

The human body builds up immunity as it is exposed to invading pathogens.

Spend time experiencing, evaluating and even enjoying rejection, for it is a critical element in your path to success.

What's Wrong With My Party?

I had gone weeks implementing the steps that John had taught me. I wanted all of this information to become part of who I truly was...and it did. I began to see huge success in my business, in my personal life and even with people who I hadn't met before. Somehow, people saw me as someone they wanted to get to know. I had people calling and asking me to go to lunch. This was a completely new concept for me. I was always the one to invite people.

Even though people invited me to lunch, I still controlled the party. I took control and listened. I controlled how long it was, and I even controlled how enjoyable the lunch was. After all, it was my party.

Life was working out pretty well, and I was enjoying myself. My boss was very happy to see who I had become and actually ended up being in my Core Network. Every once in a while, however, I would hit a snag. John and I would get together about once a week for a cup of coffee or lunch. I would always take the opportunity to ask his opinion; realizing that every time I asked anything of him, I needed to make sure that I had enough in my relationship account to withdrawal. I was so pleased with the effects of the new teaching and all the care and training that he had poured into me, that I was not sure I would ever feel as though I was ahead in that account. Even though John assured me many times that I was, I still felt like I owed him so much. He explained to me that "Mentoring" works that way and one day I would be helping others and I would understand.

He continued to instruct me in the things that he noticed needed work in my life. I was always being corrected, but I actually looked forward to it. I saw it as a chance to make sure I was still on the right path, kind of like reading a compass. I wanted to "course-correct" as much as possible, so that I didn't have a chance to get too far off my path. And, although John was always really great about training me by actually caring about me, I went through a season that I called, "My Party Flops."

As I continued to evaluate the things that were going wrong with my parties, I realized that as the host of the party, it may or may not have been my fault, but it was definitely my responsibility to fix. If your party is struggling, you may need to evaluate some of the following situations.

Too Many Connections

One main problem I had at the beginning of my journey was that I was trying to connect with too many people in too short a time. I really wanted to grow my network fast. I hoped that I could manage all of the relationships I made, but in reality, I actually sacrificed friendships for numbers. I would do a similar thing on LinkedIn and Facebook. I would connect with people but really wasn't able to work my way into their lives. John was right about this. People could tell when I was just connecting and when I really wanted to be a part of their lives. I eventually understood what John was talking about when he used to tell me that I had too many business cards after a networking event. When I tried to connect with too many people, I did not actually connect with any of them. My focus was on growing bigger and having more people in my network. After learning to slow down and be methodical about INviting, INvolving, and INvesting in people, I became better at managing relationships with more and more people at once. It was tough to keep myself from trying to meet more people, but I eventually realized I had more opportunities to meet these and other great people at the next networking event.

No Energy

One of the main things that I notice now about other people at these events is the lack of energy they seem to have. I understand it. I used to have the same problem and had to fake it too. If I am going to have a party, I am going to enjoy it. And if I am enjoying myself, it is so much easier to be full of life, full of fun, full of energy. I learned that there is really no good reason to host a party if you don't want to. Your customers, your friends and even the people who don't know you can tell that you really are not interested in being there. Unfortunately, they will determine that it is them and their company that you are not interested in. We all see things from our own points of view and most of us tend to believe negative things about ourselves. So when a person is not interested in me and what I am talking about, I tend to take that personally, even if they have other reasons for feeling that way. I later realized that people have different issues, personalities and even attention spans. I decided to host a great party with lots of energy, and hope that people would join in...and they did. If you are going to show up...show up with energy.

Trying to Impress

One of the problems you might experience when hosting your own party is that people are just not impressed with you. This problem, once realized, tends to cause us to try harder. This in turn, often seems to have the opposite effect on people. People are not impressed with people who are impressed with themselves. People want you to be impressed with them. They want you to see them, they want you to hear them, and they want you to care about them. People get impressed with you when you take the time to listen to them and even get involved in either being empathetic or helping find a solution to their situation. The more time you spend trying to impress others is time you could be using to actually work your way IN to their lives...and when you work your way IN, you will not just make an impression, you will make an impact.

No Long-Term Vision

If you really want to make an impact in someone's life, you need to make sure that you have a long-term vision for the relationship. If this is just about a sale for you, then you are going to be a salesman. If this is about having more connections on social media, then you are going to be just that...a connection. But if you plan on being a friend, then you need to plan on being a friend for life. This has nothing to do with the job you have or what you sell. This has to do with the fact that this person is going to be a good friend if you stay in the current job you have or if you change to another company years from now. Connections are easy, customers are everywhere, but friends are truly valuable, and we all could use more friends.

Under-Deliver

One of the main issues for any salesman is the conflict between sales and fulfillment. So many times I have made a deal and saw it fall apart by poor service fulfillment, bad technical support or even inferior products for my customer. When you set up a deal, it is your word to your customer and to have the whole thing fall apart due to others in your company creates a bad taste in your customer's mouth when they think of you or your company. As you create long-term friendships, so many of the imperfections in business are overlooked because your customer is now your friend. This in no way gives you the right to perform sub-par service or poor support. It is not a reason to under-deliver. In fact, it actually causes you to work harder to make things better. You tend to work harder and better for your friends. You tend to go the extra mile for your friends. You tend to take care of your friends simply because they are your friends.

When someone in your company drops the ball on one of your projects, you take control and try to fix it because this project is for a close, personal friend of yours.

Be A Giver Not A Taker

If you haven't figured it out yet, this entire book is about being a giver and not a taker. If you are going to host a party and make it all about you, your friends are going to eventually stop coming to your parties. But if you are entirely focused on your guests, they will love your parties and come back often. Givers tend to be respected for their philanthropy. Takers tend to become known for just that...taking. Spend a moment and think of people you know and place them on a line-scale between givers on one end and takers on the other. Do you see a correlation between the degree of giver that they are and the amount of enjoyment you get from being around them? Now take a moment and evaluate yourself on the same scale. When I did this little exercise, I didn't like where I landed on the scale. Then I realized that others saw me this way. I began working hard to change my attitude towards giving. I began to be a giver and not a taker.

This does not mean that you have to give away everything that you have. It does not mean that you cannot have something for yourself. If a farmer sows all of his seed, he will starve. If he turns all his seed into food, he will have no crop next year. Your giving needs to be what you determine in your heart to give. That is who you really are. If you don't like where you landed on the scale, giving more does not fix the situation. You need to change your heart and become more of a giver.

To really host a great party, make it about your friends, not about you. Be a giver, not a taker.

Relational Only When You Need Something

One of the main problems that I had early in my career was that I could really reach out and follow up when I needed something. However, I wasn't all that great at staying connected with those people who didn't order from me or didn't really benefit me. I had my customers, and I had my friends, but my customers quickly became my friends, if I ever needed something from them. This caused a lot of animosity towards me and by extension, my company. People were rarely excited to see me. Few people ever reached out to connect with me.

I had to learn how to treat everyone like a friend at all times, and the more I did, the more I realized that people treated me like a friend. The real benefit of being a good friend is that you have good friends. Friends all take care of each other and actually care about each other's business, family, health, and anything else that comes up in a friend's life.

When you are only relational as you need something, you think you have good friends, but in reality, you are

~ 118 ~

alone. Your sales, your business, your life is entirely built upon your product and service. When you go out of business, your customers may notice but will find a replacement for you.

When you are relational with everyone at all times, your sales, your business and your life are built entirely on friendships. If you are struggling, your friends will work hard to help you because that is what friends do, so...be relational at all times.

Party Favors

Just a little something to take with you!

At one of my birthday parties as a child, I noticed that my mom had bought gifts for all the other kids who were going to be there. Of course I had to complain. After all, this was my birthday and I should have been the one getting the gifts. "You always give your guests something to take with them," she said. "They are called Party Favors, and they make everybody remember your party."

Well, here are some Party Favors for you to take with you.

Where To Meet

When arranging a meeting with a person, either in your network or soon to be added to your network, your choice of venue can influence how the meeting goes. The atmosphere needs to be complimentary to your meeting. If it is too loud, you will not connect well. If there is something else for them to focus on, you may lose their attention. If you have wait staff, you will need to leave a tip and also most likely feel the pressure to leave in order to clear the table for them to get another customer in. Coffee shops can be a great alternative so long as the seating is comfortable, and the music is not too loud. Restaurants with some carpet and plastered walls will help absorb sound. You may not have anything confidential to discuss, but if you are sitting next to a loud couple or a crying baby, you could find yourself struggling to keep your friend's attention. Remember...this is your party, and you need to control it.

Create Your Own Work

You need to understand that most of the time, what you are offering is something that people have seen before. You sell insurance, they already have insurance. You sell pool services, they already have pool services.

This is where you need to shine. This is where you can come up with a different angle that they have not seen before. Come up with a reason they need you and then work to fill that need. If you are unique, people will go out of their way to find out about you. Create your own work of art in your business and simply let people know about it.

Articulate Your Story

I am sure you have practiced your 30-second pitch and probably recited it at many networking events. Your pitch is designed to let the masses know who you are and what you do. Now you need to be able to articulate your story for just one specific person...the next person you meet. Your story should be short, concise and easy to understand, but more importantly, it should come from the real you. Take some time and really think about what you would want to know about the person in your position...what matters and what doesn't? Get rid of the stuff that doesn't matter and fill the time that you have to share with something that draws out your friends and makes them want to know more. Is the name of your company important? Is your title at the company important? Would your story be more valuable to people if they heard what they needed instead of what you do?

Anyplace, Anytime

You are a networking party animal. You need to make sure that you are always ready and always available. This doesn't mean giving up time with your spouse or only focusing on work. The networking that you do should become a lifestyle, not part of your job. You can connect people at work, at home, at church and even when you go to the store. It is not so much that everyone is a target, but rather that everyone needs a friend. You can be that friend.

Never Stop Learning

You don't have to be the smartest person in the room to be the person that everyone likes. But there are plenty of opportunities to learn about your customers, clients and friends. A simple search on the internet could help you appear to be incredibly knowledgeable during the discussion. Not just about your friend, but also about their business and even about their entire industry. This may also help when you connect with another friend who ends up needing this service. Now, you are really networking.

The more people feel like you are interested in them and their business, the more they will know that you actually took the time to care about them. You may impress someone with your knowledge, but you impact them by caring.

Remember To Not Forget

We all forget things from time to time. You do not have to be perfect, but remembering someone's name, business or other pertinent information can have amazing results in strengthening your relationship. Come up with tricks to help you remember things that need to be "not forgotten."

Add family names to contacts in your phone list. During conversations with people, asking how their spouse is doing can instantly change a business call into a personal call. Remembering the names of their children is something that will set you apart form other salesmen. If they mention something that one of their children is doing, put it on your calendar and send an email or handwritten note afterwards to let them know that you thought about them and their life. Remember...people don't live to work, they work to live. Talk to them about life, not work.

Learn How To Say No

With 50 legitimate friends, your life can get very busy. If you step out to Level 2, you have 2500 friends who you have to meet for dinner, movies and even help them move into their new house. You do not have enough time. It is very important to say "No." But you have to learn how to do it correctly.

Saying "No" can be negative or it can actually be perceived as a positive position. You life is now about helping others get what they want, but find ways to help your friends in ways that you can afford, financially but also time wise.

By declining to meet when they ask, you have created an abrupt end to their line of thinking. By offering an alternative, you allow their thought process to continue and possibly be redirected. Saying "No" doesn't have to be final. Find a way to turn your "No" into an offer for something different.

A rejection of a lunch meeting might have a 30-minute meeting over a cup of coffee as a counter-offer.

Make sure you don't end a conversation, a line of thinking or even a relationship by saying "No."

Uncharted Terrain

Don't fear new ventures. Sure, life is risky, but think of all the innovators who have gone before you and boldly jumped into the uncharted terrain ahead of them. Sometimes uncharted terrain is a task; sometimes that terrain is a mentality; but sometimes that uncharted terrain is people. People can be your greatest resource and are actually vital to your success. If you were the only person on earth, you would never become a successful business person because you would have no customers; therefore, you would have no business. Oftentimes we may feel that people can be our biggest obstacles, but they can also be our greatest source of fuel for success. Step out to the edge, look out over the uncharted terrain ahead of you...and jump.

Your Silence Is Louder Than Words

Communication is a very important part of your new relationships. It is really important to be able to describe to your friends exactly what you do and how you may be able to help them. But it is actually more important to make sure you learn about them. When your friends are talking about themselves, just listen.

When you are talking, other people have the opportunity to learn something. When others are talking, you have the opportunity to learn something. And the more you learn about them, their lives and their situations, the easier it is to work your way IN.

You were given two ears and only one mouth. Could it be that listening is twice as important as talking?

Listen to what your friends are saying, and it will speak volumes about you and your friendship.

Solving The World's Problems

From time to time you will encounter a friend who has a problem that you do not have the answer to. A fantastic method of problem solving is the 10/25 Method:

Sit down and get quiet.

Get something to write with and something to write on.

Write the problem or goal at the top of the page.

Take 10 minutes and write down 25 solutions to the problem. It doesn't matter how good these solutions are, just write. Many of these will be ridiculous but write them anyway. This is brainstorming. You are almost definitely not going to come up with the answer, but this exercise will help create the mindset to think of a real solution. Often, this exercise finds a thought, that leads to the solution.

One of the advantages of the 10/25 Method is that you can share it with your friends. It can be a lot of fun to collaborate on this problem, and they will be incredibly grateful if one of the ideas leads them to a solution to their problem. At the very least, you are helping them think, empathizing with them, and being a part of their life. People will appreciate your involvement.

Lead From The Middle

Not all of us are the CEO of a business. But just because you are not the leader, doesn't mean you are not leading. Anytime someone is following you or your ideas, you are leading. In your network, you will have numerous opportunities to lead people, and when you are the leader, you have an incredible opportunity to direct people where you would like them to go. If you are a good leader, they will continue to follow you, and others will join the journey as well. If you lead poorly, you will have fewer and fewer people to lead.

~ 128 ~

Spend time making sure that you are leading your network into places that will benefit them. Then they will not only follow you, they will be there to support you as you need them.

P.L.U.S.

People Love Unselfish Service, they just do. We love the idea that people live to serve us. I love the thought that the waitress is bringing me coffee because she really wants me to have it, and not because she is getting paid to do it and definitely not for a tip. People Love Unselfish Service and are willing to pay for it...with their time, energy and money.

If you make your friends feel like you are serving them unselfishly, they will gladly return the favor, patronize your business and even become invested in your life. They will begin to care about the things that you care about because you took time to care about them.

One of the best ways to become a PLUS type person is to volunteer. Find an organization that you believe in and give them your time. Volunteering will affect your attitude with all of those around you, and your friends will see that you are actually a philanthropist, at least with your time and energy.

Sometimes, the best thing you can give to someone is
some time.

If People Love Unselfish Service, give them your best and watch them give their best back to you.

Your Party Favors

Remember, this is your party. You need to provide party favors for your guests. Always have something for your guests to take with them. Sometimes your party favor may be information. Sometimes it may be a connection or an idea. Sometimes, it may be something physical. Make sure you always give them something to remember your party and by extension you.

Connect them with someone.

Help them solve a problem.

Give them an idea for a new direction in their business.

Send a Thank You note.

Always leave them with a reminder of your great party that they attended. Make sure they want to attend another party.

Plan Your Own Party

Now it's time to launch out. You have made your list. You have separated them into groups, and you have begun reciting their names and thinking about them everyday. Now it is time to work you way IN.

It is time to host your own party.

Remember the party rules:

INvite

INvolve

INvest

before you can

INvoice.

Now...

Works Cited

Clay, Robert. "Why You Must Follow Up Leads." Marketing Donut. Atom Small Business Experts, Web. July 2, 2018.

Tarcomnicu, Felix. "27 Amazing Sales Facts that Will Change How You Sell." B2C: Business 2 Community. Brightinfo, March 1, 2016. Web. July 2, 2018.

Frost, Aja. "75 Mind-Blowing Sales Statistics that Will Help You Sell Smarter in 2018." HubSpot. HubSpot, October 10, 2017. Web. July 2, 2018

Also by Brad C. Engel &
Neil F. Anderson

Limitless Connections is a fantastic leap into the world of Networking and lays out a specific plan for becoming a networking professional.

"A fantastic read..."

"Great Information and fantastic teaching on implementing it"

Also by Brad C. Engel

Goodnight Gorgeous is a fifteen year journey to real healing of a broken heart through Love. From a bad situation to a great marriage, it is a fantastic picture of how God loves us and will never give up on us.

"This book will challenge you to love your spouse the way Christ loves you, and shows you how."

"An absolute must read for anyone who is in a relationship, wants to be, or has one falling apart."

Bethel1808 Publishers

Brad C. Engel and **Neil F. Anderson** are available for speaking engagements and book signings.

For more information, contact them through the publisher at:
Brad@Bethel1808.com
Neil@Bethel1808.com

Bethel1808 exists to help authors at every stage of the process. If you are interested in other books by the Bethel1808 family of authors, please visit:
Bethel1808.com

If you have a book in you and are interested in working with Bethel1808, please contact us at our website or email us at:
Authors@Bethel1808.com

About the Authors

Brad C. Engel is the author of *Goodnight Gorgeous* and *Limitless Connections*. He is a motivational speaker and communications trainer for private companies and non-profit groups. Brad and his beautiful wife Laura, live in the Dallas/Ft. Worth area.

Neil F. Anderson is a Business Development Professional and inspirational speaker in the Dallas/Ft. Worth area. He is the author of *Limitless Connections* and lives in the Dallas/Ft. Worth area with his beautiful wife, Dorothy.

Made in the USA
Columbia, SC
18 July 2018